Michael J. Mayer, Ed.D.

Better Sex
Through Deeper
Emotional Intimacy

ISBN: 1478341440

ISBN-13: 9781478341444

Library of Congress Control Number: 2012914004

CreateSpace Independent Publishing Platform

North Charleston, South Carolina

Author's note

The names and identities of the people in this book have been disguised to such an extensive degree that any resemblance to any person, living or dead, is purely coincidental. Most of the cases represent composites of many clients with similar problems. I have done this to protect client confidentiality.

Acknowledgements

This book was made possible by the people who put trust in me to help them deal with and appreciate their lives in new and better ways. To these people and to my wife, family, and friends, I say thank you from my heart and soul. Most importantly, I thank you, God, for your example of unconditional love for us.

Better Sex
Through Deeper Emotional Intimacy

Introduction

Part One

This section is about the "basic qualities" an individual should use and integrate within themselves to help them understand the people they love.

> **Dynamic One: Flexibility**
>
> **Dynamic Two: Other Focused**
>
> **Dynamic Three: Communicate / Listen**

Part Two

This section is about an individual understanding what he/she stands for as a person who is trying to love someone else. These qualities are very important to possess.

> **Dynamic Four: Boundaries**
>
> **Dynamic Five: Spirituality**
>
> **Dynamic Six: Commitment**

Part Three

This section focuses on an advanced understanding of the self and the willingness of the self to become emotionally involved with someone else.

> **Dynamic Seven: Vulnerability**
>
> **Dynamic Eight: Trust**
>
> **Dynamic Nine: Forgiveness**

Part Four

This section focus on achieving the goal. The goal is to be emotionally, physically, and spiritually fulfilled in ways that culminate in a committed love.

> **Committed Love and Better Physical Intimacy**

Mayer, 2012

İntroduction

Can you love me forever?

As a psychologist, over the years of my involvement with the lives of children, families, couples, and individuals, I have found that relationships are very important to the mental well-being of these individuals. Relating with the various people in our lives is challenging but very rewarding when appropriately connected to the other individuals with whom we come in contact. Relating to your marriage partner by incorporating aspects of the nine dynamics in this book into your lives as a couple will be the added strength to your physical attraction to each other. In simpler terms, BETTER SEX.

From birth to death, many people will cross our paths. We will touch many lives, and many others will touch our lives. Each connection to another human being leaves a mark, a memory, a feeling. We are not always aware of the impact these people are making in the life we are currently living. Of course, without a doubt, the most influential people in our early existence are our parents.

Parents are the reason we exist. Parents pass on the family biology, the genetics of our unique makeup. Our parents are our teachers in life, our first instructors on how to cope with the challenges of growing up. Parents are our first mentors.

Over the years of helping children and adults of varied ages, I have concluded that most people think their way of acting is the right way of acting. Their perception of how they interact with others is considered by them as adequate all the way. They feel that it is the best way they know how to accomplish the task or challenge at hand. This is true for most parents. As they pass on their beliefs regarding parenting, they do truly believe in what they are doing. This does not mean that their style is effective or even appropriate, but in their minds and at this time with the knowledge they have, their parenting actions are appropriate. After all, their parenting is probably a version of their parents' style of parenting.

The parenting style of our parents is then passed down to their children (us). Not only do our parents leave us with their parenting style, but they also leave us with messages on how to relate to others. Our parents taught us about loving others, self-acceptance, conflict resolution, attitudes about life, about moral values, and on and on. This can be a scary thought.

Parents are not perfect teachers. They also are learning about life and about being a parent. As many people have told me, babies do not come with a set of instructions. Even if they did, the instructions would be heavily influenced by the hand-me-down biochemistry of the parents.

Next to the influence of parents on our life comes the influence of relatives, teachers, religious leaders, peers, friends, and others. All of these people have had a significant impact on our way of learning and on our way of interacting with others. In my thirty years of helping people understand their emotions relating to life's personal issues for them, their tales of their past are so influenced by their parents and by those people that they allowed to touch their life. Those people of influence had significant roles in these people's current way of interacting with others.

We learn how to interact with others through our past interactions with significant people. We do not often think of these influences on our behavior as we interact with those currently in our lives. So what we have learned in the past is often what we do in the present. Are we aware of how we affect those with whom we interact daily?

Why am I reminding you of the role of your parents in your life and the role of other past significant people in your life? I am doing this because without a reminder of your past influences, you may forget that the way you chose to do things today is highly influenced by your past. These past influences may not allow you to be flexible enough or "other-centered" enough to challenge your interactions with others to see if other ways of responding may be more appropriate or more effective. Responding more effectively with your marriage partner will allow you the intimacy that results in BETTER SEX.

Challenging the way you see the world and the way you interact with others is important in your relationship with others, especially the relationship with your significant other. The patterns of people interacting with others are inherited and learned. You need to be aware of what patterns you may have inherited or what patterns you may have learned. Who has influenced you?

Ineffectual relationships can and do affect our lives in many ways. As a psychologist, I spend a lot of time helping people sort out their relationships with others. Many clients start with their current relationships with their children or with their significant others. I hear about poor or ineffective relationships with a boss or coworker, with a friend or neighbor. Then there is the relationship you have with yourself: the way you accept your personal strengths and weaknesses.

We do not live in this world alone. We have to interact with those in the world around us. It is important to understand ourselves in relation to the various interactions we have with others.

It is very common for people to ask me for help with a relationship in their life. It generally starts with asking me for help with their children or with their significant other. The specifics of the problem in the relationship can be very complex or seem very simple on the surface. Whatever the case, it has bothered the person enough that he/she seeks help. The child-parent relationship problem is not the focus of this book. Nor is the person's relationship with his/her boss the main focus, even though those work relationships do have a direct connection to your relationship with your significant other. I do work with parents, families, work-related issues, personal issues, and a myriad of other concerns, but my focus here is to help us understand some key elements—some key dynamics—that I have found over the years to be helpful in couples relating in a long-term, committed love relationship.

When couple after couple and individual after individual kept coming to see me to complain about their unhappiness in their specific relationship or relationships, I began to take note of the reasons for their unhappiness. The specific reasons for dissatisfaction were numerous in nature and in the ways they were being expressed. I took note of these, and, in so doing over the years, I began formulating some of what I call dynamics" that were significant to the success of the relationships. These dynamics negatively impacted a relationship if they were not appropriately addressed. *What is interesting about these dynamics is they are very simply described, but often the individual was unwilling to embrace the effort needed to integrate them into his/her ways of behaving and interacting. This unwillingness reduces the chance for emotional intimacy that can bring about BETTER SEX.*

I like to challenge people to grow in positive ways—to challenge themselves to learn new and more effective ways of acting, thinking, and feeling. These dynamics discussed in this book, if appropriately applied in your life, will bring about a happier and a longer-lasting, meaningful relationship for you and your significant other. This adds to the emotional intimacy needed for BETTER SEX.

However, to make the relationship effective, these dynamics must be a part of both people involved in the relationship. Practicing these dynamics as an individual can make you more content as an individual, but to improve a specific relationship, both of you must incorporate these dynamics into your lives.

Patterns of behavior run deep. Ways of acting seldom change without a reason to change. Too many people say, "I am who I am" or "Accept me for who I am." We do not change people; they have to do that for themselves. So my challenge to my couple clients is to have them become aware of what they need to change in themselves to make their relationships better. Only if they are willing to change themselves first will the other person be willing to change. The key is for both to be willing to change themselves in meaningful ways simultaneously as they become aware of the wants of their partner—wants that are realistic and meaningful for the relationship as a whole.

The goal of these dynamics is to allow and help couples to become emotionally more intimate in their relationships. I am often asked about intimacy and what it takes to make a couple-relationship more intimate. The question of intimacy arises often as a result of a failing sexual relationship. One or both partners realize that physical intercourse is dwindling or, by the time I see them in therapy, nonexistent. For some, this lack of physical closeness has just started, and the couple was aware that they needed help in repairing the relationship. For others, there had not been any sexual intimacy for years. In the latter case, infidelity and/or the threat of divorce made them check out therapy before they called it quits.

In talking with the couples about the history of their relationship, the pair often became aware that the lack of physical/sexual closeness was tied into their lack of emotional intimacy. To the surprise of some, this lack of feeling of emotional closeness had never been strong over the years. Many never fully understood the meaning of emotional closeness. When they were first engaged and then married, they felt close to each other; it seemed like this was the "real deal" of love. They were physically "madly" in love. They wanted to be together forever. They were truly in love. Yes, there were some differences, but they knew they could work these out in time. Love, at times, can be blind.

How many of us really understand what it means to be in love? As asked earlier, "Where did we learn how to love?" When did we understand the dynamics that make for a deep, long-lasting, and committed relationship? What are the dynamics that help a relationship be emotionally intimate? What are the dynamics that help the relationship in ways that result in BETTER SEX?

In our twenties, are we at a high-enough level of self-understanding, let alone other-understanding, to choose a partner for life? Marriage statistics say we have a fifty-fifty chance of not getting divorced. What happens in a marriage that allows us to give up on the person we thought we were deeply in love with... the person of our dreams?

I have heard so many reasons given as to why couples wanted a divorce. The list is as unique as each couple's history and circumstances. Some basic causes, as stated by individuals within a committed relationship, were an affair; a boring relationship; a lack of closeness or time spent together; a lack of personal control of feelings, such as anger; too much criticism; financial instability; a partner wanted too much sex; gained too much weight; hated the animals; was too irresponsible; had no sense of humor; smelled funny; was addicted to porn, gambling, spending, alcohol, or drugs; was too lazy; loved him/herself too much; was too self-centered; too religious; had no religious beliefs; he/she just didn't want to be married, and on and on.

What happened to that emotional commitment? What happened to "until death do us part?" Yes, there are meaningful reasons why some marriages do not make it, but I doubt that this is true for all 50 percent of those who divorced.

We can challenge and try to understand all the unique and varied reasons couples divorce, but this may be too complicated and not very useful. It may focus too much on the negative. Instead, I have focused on where we need to place our emphasis in a committed relationship. I have experienced, with my clients, some very effective ways of interacting in a relationship that produces emotional intimacy, which leads to a deeper spiritual and physical intimacy, which leads to sustained commitment to the vow to stay together.

These effective ways of interacting will be called dynamics. These dynamics will challenge you in ways to become a better partner, and when you both incorporate these dynamics in your relationship, your relationship will become a better-committed relationship.

The added benefit to incorporating aspects of these dynamics into your lives as a couple will be an increase in your physical attraction to each other. In simpler terms, BETTER SEX.

Yes, better emotional intimacy has been reported by most couples to have impacted their sexual lives in stronger and more meaningful ways. So why wait? Let's proceed to learn and/or relearn these dynamics that can lead to an emotionally, spiritually, and physically better and long-lasting interaction with the person you love.

Remember, better sex comes through deeper emotional intimacy!

Part One

This section is about the "basic qualities" an individual should understand and integrate within themselves to use in understanding the person he/she loves.

Dynamic One: Flexibility

Dynamic Two: Other Focused

Dynamic Three: Communicate / Listen

Dynamic One:
Flexibility

Isn't the world according to me?

"Flexibility of perception can lead to encouraging in yourself an openness on all fronts—physical, emotional, intellectual, spiritual—that denies difference and defies the practice of exclusion." (Dorwick, 1996, p. 86)

I have chosen to begin teaching these varied dynamics with a dynamic I call flexibility. As with many words, it has a different meaning to different people. I will never understand what you mean by the word *flexibility* unless I ask you. Your meaning of the word was learned from parents or a teacher or by your personal experience of being flexible. Thus written, I will define my definition of the word flexible as I use it within the context of a relationship.

To be flexible in a relationship means to be able to look at your chosen partner's words and actions with an open viewpoint. You are able to look at both sides of a statement or action without first shutting down because it disagrees with the way you think and/or feel about the statement. You are able to listen, ask questions, and then decide together on a course of action, not always as you would prefer. You become more willing to see the world in a different way. It will not always be the world according to the way you see it, nor will it always be the world according to the way your partner sees it. You both are willing to intellectually and emotionally remove the rigidity of how you think and feel about something where disagreement is common.

A simple example is the couple who argues over a method of disciplining the children. One believes that soda is not bad for the kids, while the other believes it should never cross their lips. This is a minor disagreement for the two of you, but it is major for the children. The wall is up; the stances are firm; there is no giving in.

Remembering that you want to learn the dynamic of being flexible, you both should be willing to try the 2-2-4 method in solving your differences. I have devised this method over the years to help many couples resolve conflicts.

For approximately two minutes, one person states his/her viewpoint without the other person interrupting. At the end of the two minutes, the person who was listening summarizes the other person's views on the disputed topic. Now the listener has an opportunity to state his/her viewpoint for the next two minutes, after which the first person summarizes what he/she heard.

Once this process is completed, the two people have four minutes to brainstorm new solutions to resolve the conflict. All ideas are acceptable. Leave no option out. When finished with options, agree to select one to try. Give it a try, and then evaluate its success.

On some very difficult conflicts, it might be necessary to do one of the following:

1. Agree to disagree, and start a "give-in" list where one of you agrees to be first to give in to the standoff. Note the date and the topic that was conceded.

When the next unresolved topic arises after an unsuccessful 2-2-4 attempt, the other person agrees to give in. Keep this "give-in" list as a reference for the future to avoid discussing who gave in the last time. I have known the "who gave in last time" argument to become more heated than the disagreement that caused the fight in the first place.

2. Another way to resolve an unsuccessful 2-2-4 method attempt is to agree upon a third party to offer his/her solution to the unresolved conflict. You agree ahead of time that this person's solution will be accepted. Examples would be to use a financial planner or banker for a financial question, or a pastor or spiritual leader for a spiritual question.

Being flexible is not always the seemingly natural way to look at a conflict in a relationship. But without this willingness to try and work on flexibility, you might as well have married yourself. That way you would always be in agreement with your views; there's no one to disagree with you. How exciting (or boring) would that be?

Being flexible allows you to avoid circular thinking, where the mind repeats the same answers and solutions to problems. We often aren't flexible enough to allow new solutions into the picture. Another factor that can influence our stubbornness in allowing new solutions or new ideas into our response is that somewhere in the past the solution worked for us. We then tend to think that the same solution will work every time. Our inflexibility gets reinforced. Because the solution met our need at that time, however, does not mean it is always the most appropriate way to respond. Life is more complex than a single solution. What may work in one situation may not work in another. What works with one child may not work with another child.

Rules for children need to be very consistent. Some of these rules may and should change as the children get older. For example, bed times change with age. Curfews change with age and individual maturity. These challenges with children need to be looked at with the flexible view of the child's growth, emotionally and intellectually.

In marriage, flexibility is a must when disagreeable situations and conflicts arise. Resolving most of the major differences between couples should be completed *before* marriage. Changing something important in your potential marriage partner after you are married is much more difficult. Issues of religious or spiritual preferences need to be resolved before you commit for life. Emotional intimacy issues need to be discussed early on. Financial spending should be in order. The list of possible disagreements goes on. How you resolve these differences will give you an idea of how you will resolve other issues after you have vowed to love each other for life. Solving your conflicts will necessitate the use of flexibility.

You should want to be flexible with the person you love—you should want to understand his viewpoint, her way of thinking and acting. You should want to find a compromise of the different ways the two of you look at things. This is the person you should want to allow into your heart and soul as he or she lets you into his or her heart and soul.

Flexibility brings you emotionally closer to the person you love. You are looking at the world together through two pairs of eyes, not just one. As you bend together—it takes both—you free yourselves to be more intimate emotionally, and this brings about a better physical (sexual) response between the two of you. Those moments of agreement are touching.

To allow this flexibility, it helps for the two of you to possess some of the other dynamics, which we'll discuss in the following chapters.

Flexibility was deemed very important to one of my middle-aged clients. She sees its importance in her relationship with her significant other.

She states, "Flexibility in any relationship is essential. One must not only know themselves how to do this, but know and understand the other person. Flexibility means that one person's needs temporarily might easily take priority over the other's. It might mean delaying our own needs or sense of gratification.

"For example, if my normal routine is to get up early and do homework when everyone is asleep, and then suddenly a family member's schedule changes and he or she is now up early as well, it may require flexibility on my part to reanalyze my day to meet the needs of this family member. This might mean that I begin doing homework in the evening, when the family member is not yet home from work. This allows me time with my loved one, as well as time for the study atmosphere that I needed. It is a matter of re-prioritizing. Are you flexible enough to not care whether the toilet paper roll comes out over the top or underneath?

"Being able to be flexible allows the other person to feel special and important, and he or she will have a sense of security about the relationship. This security has to do with knowing that although life presents constant change, the core relationship with each other will not change. An issue in a relationship could arise when one person is not able or willing to be flexible."

Such wise words from this person. I want to underscore her last statement that both must be able and willing to be flexible. This is about a relationship, not just you.

Be willing to get into other people's shoes, walk their walk, and see what they see before you present your version of the world to them.

QUESTIONS

Flexibility

Do you look at both sides of an issue?

ALWAYS | | | | | NEVER

Are you willing to check out both sides of a situation by actively asking for clarity?

ALWAYS | | | | | NEVER

Are you willing to come to a middle road on issues of difference?

ALWAYS | | | | | NEVER

Dynamic Two:
Other-Focused

You mean I have to think of someone else?

"The successful resolution of the intimacy crisis involves achieving a balance between taking care of oneself and actively caring for others. Those who fail to strike this balance either focus exclusively on the needs of others, thus neglecting their own needs, or are self-centered and have little room for concern about others." (Corey, 2011, p. 147)

"Not emphasized in the attachment literature, but persuasive to me, is that the more partners can realize how much they are shaped by each other and how much of their supposed 'independent selves' is located in shared experience, the more deeply attached they feel." (Gerson, 2007, p. 254)

To be flexible will probably require possessing some of the characteristics of this next dynamic, being other-focused—allowing the focus of life to shift toward someone else, in this case, to your committed partner. You are willing to realize (or already know) that being with someone you deeply love 24–7 requires a special consideration on your part regarding the well-being of that person. *You have to learn to think for two, sometimes for the first time in your life.* Did you grow up thinking about how you affected others? Did you learn as a child to share and be considerate of others? Did you see your parents being considerate of each other's feelings as well as your feelings?

I have worked with many people over the course of thirty years, each person being uniquely different. Seeing these people as individuals who were concerned about their panic attacks, their obsessive thinking, their depression, or other personal conflicts usually included their relationships to and with others. Their problems tended to focus on their getting better, but part of the issues also involved the people in their lives, whether they be parents, siblings, spouses, partners, children, or coworkers/bosses. It is difficult to have a problem that does not somehow involve others.

Then I have the couples who come to see me with their relationship issues together. There is something between them that is not working. In many cases, the problem is with some characteristic in their partner...something that became intolerable over time. They want it fixed. Often, they want the other person fixed. It really helps when the couple realizes that both need to change. Or even better, they want to know what each of them must do within themselves to make the relationship work. They take ownership of their parts in the decline of the marriage or partnership.

I seldom hear a client who comes into marital or relationship counseling say to me, "I want help making myself a better partner for the one I love." Wouldn't that be nice? This would only work if both in the relationship felt the same way. Too often, we start life protecting ourselves from the challenges of daily existence. Somewhere in the early stages of life, we have the opportunity to let others—especially our caretakers, our parents—into our minds, souls, and hearts. As a child, this is a more natural time to learn to care and trust in others. Having loving and trusting parents helps in this process. Our parents teach us that being loved and loving in return has its own wonderful meaning. Unfortunately, not all parents know how to appropriately and effectively love their children. This ability (or lack of ability) to love others, other than ourselves, is often first learned from our parents. What we have learned early on is then passed along to others whose lives we touch (or fail to touch).

My point is that being other-centered in a relationship has its roots in our earliest experiences in life. These experiences, unless altered, will continue to influence our willingness and ability to think of how our actions affect others and our ability to care enough to be concerned about how we express our emotional closeness to others.

As one client so clearly stated in response to the question of what he wanted in his thirty-five-year marriage, "I want for both of us spiritual, mental, and physical warmth and support. We should love and respect each other for who we are, not who we want the other to become. We should want each other in our lives to share everything we are with each other. There is nothing we won't do for each other's happiness. The effort is not an issue, because we love each other. Always wanting and trying to be better and to help the other to feel better, to pick each other up when we fall. We should feel confident that we are in each other's corner. We feel confident that we won't diss each other; we will always be there when the need arises and work together as a lifelong team."

To hear this from this man as he spoke to his wife of thirty-five years warmed my heart. But it takes work by both parties to live focused on each other's well-being.

Here are two examples of people who have trouble considering the needs of their partners as an important part of their decisions.

Jill is now thirty-two. She was an only child and grew up in a family where her parents were also only children. She loves life. She loves being the center of attention. As she has grown in age, she has become independent and able to get her way in most everything she tries or wants. She has learned how to get her way in life.

Jill has one problem. She has difficulty in relationships. Her independent thinking skills are good, but she is not willing to look at others' viewpoints. She sets her goals and expectations, but is not willing to consider other options. It is her way or the highway for those trying to get close to her. When asked if she cares about others, the answer is "yes…if they agree with my way of thinking and feeling." Until Jill is willing to look at and consider what others are feeling and thinking, she may continue to have problems in relationships.

Charles is over sixty and has been married and divorced two times. He is currently in a relationship and experiencing the same difficulty. His partner keeps telling him that he seems too focused on his own needs and wants and doesn't recognize or hear any of her concerns or what she might expect from him in their relationship. Charles is perplexed and wants to know what he is doing that makes the woman in his life feel unloved. Charles and I started digging into his past relationships, his present relationship, and his most important relationship—the one with his parents. I will simplify what we discovered. Charles was brought up in a family that prided themselves on individual accomplishments. Both parents were professional and spent over sixty hours a week apiece working to become successful. The parents encouraged their children to become successful, independent professionals who used their talents to the fullest. Time spent together as a family was very limited. The parents were too busy to model emotional intimacy. Showing emotional closeness to the children was minimal—more expectation was placed on getting chores done, getting good grades, and staying out of trouble. Only achievements were recognized. Except for anger, emotions were not expressed. The love in some form was there, but it was never outwardly expressed unless someone was hurt and getting over the hurt and moving on was the "order of the day."

Charles felt that he learned how to be strong, how take care of himself, and how to work hard to achieve and be successful,

25

which he did well. He admitted that being emotionally close to someone was nice for a while, but he never considered it as important as being a good provider and being successful as a professional. Unfortunately, the women he chose in life wanted emotional intimacy. They had grown up in homes that displayed emotional warmth as a part of the family unity. Charles was able to show enough closeness in the beginning—a closeness driven by a physical/sexual drive to win the hearts of the women he loved. But this level of emotional closeness was not the longer-lasting and deeper emotional intimacy wanted by the women in his life. Charles did not know how to achieve a deeper level of emotional closeness with women in his life. He couldn't figure out why these women did not appreciate him for his being able to provide for them and be good to them and treat them well. These are great qualities, but they lack the emotional intimacy that a partner may want included as an important part of a relationship. Interestingly, not all partners want a significant level of closeness. They are not willing to take the emotional risk. After all, it hurts if you have it and then lose it.

Charles was willing to work on his personal growth in the area of emotional other-centeredness, looking at how his self-focus often left the other person in his life feeling alone and forgotten.

In general, other-focused people are willing to look at how they can better themselves in order to make their relationship better.

They are willing to analyze their own actions, and to check them out before they act. Other-focused people try to look at the world through two pairs of eyes, theirs and their partner's. There is a true intent to be aware of their own actions and words. It is fine to have your own beliefs and actions, but it is important to add another dimension to your thinking by checking out how people are being affected by your beliefs and actions. Have some empathy. Can you be other-focused enough as a guy to watch a chick flick with your wife in a theater without looking around to see who may see you?

When we become too self-driven and self-wanting, we begin to lose important emotional connections with others and become superficial in our relationships. If our actions affect someone negatively (even when we may not agree that our actions warranted that reaction), we should care enough that someone hurts because of our actions and be willing to make a change.

This other-focused dynamic can be taught to our children as they observe our behavior toward them and others. Handing this dynamic down to our children is a very precious gift of a lifetime.

Compatibility in marriage can be greatly enhanced by attempting to understand our partner's preferences and ways of doing things. These actions can include:

- Being on time to meet our spouse and calling if we are going to be late

- Paying attention to his/her preferences when trying to make a choice

- Trying to understand his/her point of view first before we state ours

- Being willing to look at better ways to respond to our spouse

- Finding activities to do together that we both like

- Finding ways to help our spouse when he/she seems overwhelmed

- Being willing to look at our role when our partner is frustrated with us

- Being less defensive when we disagree

If you think of others, it can help you focus less on concerns that tend to excessively bother you. Thinking of others and how you affect them can also help you put your concerns in better perspective. Refocus on ways to compromise and finding different solutions.

Being other-centered helps us live in this world of people.

QUESTIONS

Other-Focused

When you speak to
the one you love, are   **ALWAYS** | | | | | **NEVER**
you aware of how your
words affect them?

If you are aware of how
your words/actions
affect the one you love,
do you take the time   **ALWAYS** | | | | | **NEVER**
to avoid inappropriate
and ineffective com-
munication that would
unnecessarily hurt your
partner?

Do you think of the
other person during   **ALWAYS** | | | | | **NEVER**
the day in a positive
manner?

Is your partner's input equal to yours when input is given?

ALWAYS | | | | | **NEVER**

Dynamic Three: Communicate/ Listen

Is that really what you meant?

"Basic listening skills are also important contributors to intimate experiences. Basic listening skills involve the ability to attend, paraphrase, reflect the other's feelings, and give feedback in a constructive manner...Many people are not aware that how they listen shuts down communication." (Carlson and Sperry, 1998, p. 16)

"Communication is fundamental to human interaction and intimate couple relationships, in part because communication is a tool for knowing or emotionally connecting with one another… Communication between intimate partners is more than words—it involves establishing an emotional connection." (Wiley, 2007)

Where would any self-help book be without mentioning the most commonly agreed-upon issue in any relationship: the lack of effective communication and listening? In most marriages, this issue is mentioned as being a concern needing attention. Interestingly, we all feel we know how to communicate, and we all listen when spoken to. But, on the contrary, we do not do this very effectively.

Fred and Nancy lived as a couple for more than thirty years before they came to see me about their marital issues. As it turns out, communication was a concern in their marriage. They either verbally disagreed with each other, or they misunderstood what the other was saying. A simple, "I will see you in a bit," ended in a fight because "a bit" to one was a ten- or fifteen-minute wait, while it meant at least a sixty-minute wait to the other. They never bothered to check with each other what "a bit" meant.

Each assumed the other knew. As a result, they made a lot of false assumptions about the meanings of their spoken words. Fred and Nancy agreed they needed to practice better communication and listening skills. The skills they were learning in marriage therapy were also skills they realized they could use with their children and in their respective places of work.

When I write about needing good communication skills in marriage, it reminds me of a dear couple that I worked with in marriage counseling when I first started practice. They admitted that they had the poorest communication skills of any couple they knew. No matter what came out of the mouth of either one of them, the other disagreed. I found this hard to believe, but they proved to me it was true. As an assignment for them between sessions, I asked them to make a list of the things they had agreed upon during the course of their marriage. I was hoping this list would make them realize that they did have things in common; that there were commonalities between them, some good experiences they shared together. The next session came, and the couple brought in their list of agreed-upon issues, experiences, beliefs, and anything they wanted to put on the list. They handed me the list. To my surprise, it had only one item. It was simply stated that the only thing they agreed upon during their married life was that she made the best chicken and dumplings of anyone in the county. Their eighteen-year-old daughter verified that truly this was the only thing her parents had ever agreed upon. What a challenge it was for them to learn how to communicate about issues and about their differences as individuals trying to live together in a meaningful way.

Communication in marriage is imperative if a marriage is to survive the challenging world of today. Never assume you know and understand what is being communicated to you. Check out what you hear by letting the other person know what you heard them express to you. It doesn't hurt to repeat to your partner your interpretation of what he/she said, and then ask him/her if this was what he/she meant. *Remember, it is your perception of his/her perception of what he/she said that leaves a lot of room for error.*

Good communication is about clarity of thought and feeling, not trying to convince someone to do it your way. That will be his or her choice.

Couples can be individually biased in what they want to hear from their partners. *Listening with accuracy and understanding is a true art.* Tell a story that lasts about five minutes to a group of about twenty people, and then ask them to write down what they heard. You will be amazed at what they put down and what they thought they heard.

Words take on so many meanings. How about the example of the husband who, when asked the name of his wife's favorite flower, replied, "Gold Medal?" He was so proud of his answer, until he looked over at his wife's frown.

Communication and listening at work is also important in job satisfaction and personal productivity. This example extends the importance of knowing how to communicate.

Brian, who was in his early forties, lost his job due to the poor economy. He had enjoyed his job as a parts manager in an auto dealership. He searched and searched for a job, until he found a job distributing products to homes and stores. The job was a job and Brian was eager for a paycheck, so he took the job without asking many questions. The company needed someone who presented well and had a good work ethic. Details and expectations were not clearly communicated. Within months, Brian started to hate going to work, became depressed, and lost his drive to be productive. In talking with Brian, it became evident that he hated the "cold-calling" sales part of the job. He felt that trying to sell something to a total stranger was more than he could do. He admitted that he was too shy and too insecure to do what was expected of him. This is a good example of ineffective communication on both sides, the employer and the employee.

Communication at work is just as vital to the success of a business as it is to the success of a marriage. Knowing what is expected of you at work and having the tools and skills to accomplish these expectations are two of the most important questions employees want answered from their employers. Isn't it true that knowing the expectations of your partner in marriage and having the ability for each of you to meet these expectations are very important questions to be discussed and answered?

Be aware of how your words affect others. Your intention should be to effectively state your question or make your statement without putting the listener down or being inappropriately critical. You can tell a person anything without him/her reacting negatively to your words if you are careful how you state your thoughts. It is not only the words you use but also the appropriate tone of those words. If you are really good at communicating with words, you could politely tell a person to figuratively "go jump in a lake" and they would say "thank you."

Asking questions about a statement made to you is important in your understanding of what is being said to you. Find out more of your partner's meaning to the words spoken. Asking questions is always a good way to continue a conversation. Declarative statements or statements of fact can shut down discussions.

For example, if Cheryl says she wants a blue car and it sounds like this is a "no budge" statement, for you to make a "no budge" reply (for example, saying that red is the color of your choice), the most likely outcome is a negative attitude on both sides. It could possibly have had a different outcome if you had asked Cheryl a question about her blue-car preference: "Would you consider a different color?" You may still be shut down, but your odds are better that she might be willing to consider a different color. Why not try? Generally speaking, people like to be asked, not told. Couples like to shortcut a discussion by making statements rather than being more open-ended in making decisions. Would you prefer to be asked, not told? It really works when both of you ask each other what he/she prefers. Decide together.

I like questions similar to the following:

- "I have a suggestion; would you like to hear it?"

- "Do you mind if I ask you...?"

- "Have you ever thought of...?"

- "Would you consider...?"

- "What a great idea! I have some questions about it; do you mind if I ask you?"

Realistically, you can't do this every time someone makes a statement. Save this tool for the important issues and discussions.

I like couples to live with the idea that each of them should make it a positive habit to be aware of how the words that come out of their mouths will affect the other person. If the words seem hurtful, change them before you verbalize them. Think before you speak! If you have already slipped and verbally hurt the other person, apologize and rephrase your words more appropriately. It is never too late to apologize—even days later. Haven't you heard some of this before? Did you listen? Did you actually follow the advice?

Good communication and accurate listening can make our lives more enjoyable, more productive, more meaningful, and more intimate. Good communication and accurate listening are great ways to increase emotional intimacy, which directly increases physical intimacy. Good communication keeps your spouse from feeling that the pet goldfish is a better communicator than you.

Good communication and accurate listening can be destroyed by self-centeredness, inflexible thinking, stubbornness, impatience, and by believing that the world should believe, act, and feel just like you believe, act, and feel. Just a reminder: the world is not just according to you. Our way of believing and acting is not always the best way just because it has been working for us. Be willing to communicate and be open to new suggestions and new solutions. Our world can become very small if we live life only out of our limited thinking and out of our unwillingness to change.

We can be our own worst enemies when we open our mouths to speak and when we close our minds when we listen.

Speak with clarity and listen attentively. That brings about intimacy.

QUESTIONS

Communicate/Listen

Can you openly and appropriately express your positive and negative feelings to the one you love?

ALWAYS | | | | | **NEVER**

When listening to the one you love, can you accurately repeat what you heard?

ALWAYS | | | | | **NEVER**

Do you weigh your words before you speak your thoughts and before you respond to what you heard?

ALWAYS | | | | | **NEVER**

Part Two

This section is about an individual understanding what he/she stands for as a person who is trying to love someone else. These qualities are very important to possess.

> **Dynamic Four: Boundaries**
>
> **Dynamic Five: Spirituality**
>
> **Dynamic Six: Commitment**

Dynamic Four: Boundaries

Do I have to set limits on my behavior?

"Healthy boundary practice establishes the middle ground between our feeling too vulnerable and feeling invulnerable, between wanting to express too much and not wanting to express anything at all. A healthy boundary creates controlled vulnerability." (Mellody Freundlich, 2004, p. 54)

"Any confusion of responsibility and ownership in our lives is a problem of boundaries. Just as homeowners set physical property lines around their land, we need to set mental, physical, emotional, and spiritual boundaries for our lives to help us distinguish what is our responsibility and what isn't." (Cloud and Townsend, 2007, p. 10)

Keith lives life to the fullest. He stays up late at night to read and drinks alcohol until he falls asleep. He eats more food than is necessary and continues to gain useless weight. He spends too many hours at his job trying to do too much in too short a time. He continues to push himself into ill health due to his lack of setting personal boundaries on his lifestyle.

Jack, on the other hand, keeps himself very fit, controls his food and alcohol consumption, and generally maintains a physically healthy lifestyle. He has been married to Julie for the past ten years. Jack and Julie are a well-respected couple in their community. They are very social and spend a lot of time going to community events, parties, and inviting friends to their home. All seems well on the surface. Boredom, however, is a problem for Jack. He wants more action in his life. He wants the challenge of being around women. He desires to be physically intimate with other women. He sees nothing wrong with an occasional fling, as long as his wife doesn't find out. He believes that since his wife doesn't like sex as often as he wants it, he will quietly fill that need elsewhere. At least, he feels, he is staying married to Julie. Jack does not have a boundary on infidelity.

Margaret is happily married to Jason. They both are still in love after twelve years. They enjoy each other's company; they are physically (sexually) compatible for the most part; they enjoy sports together; and they love their children. Margaret sees nothing wrong in their marriage. Jason, on the other hand, is having a serious problem with the amount of money Margaret spends on unnecessary items each month. Margaret is always finding good deals on jewelry or expensive items for their newly remodeled house. Jason is concerned, as his income (she chose not to work outside the home) cannot match her spending. Margaret has no desire to spend less. She wants Jason to move up the ladder at work and earn more money for the family. After all, her friends spend more than she does and this bothers her. Margaret's dad always let her mom buy anything she wanted. Margaret feels justified in her spending. She does not like having a limit on what she spends. Spending makes her happy, and this is good for Jason.

The examples above should show us that boundaries and limits are needed in life and in a marriage. Learning to set effective boundaries must start with yourself when you are young. Learning to set these boundaries early in life can be a great asset for you later. Everyone needs boundaries to help us function better in life.

As a child, you should have learned to say "no" to some of life's wants. You should be teaching your children time limits on their use of video games, the Internet, and cell phones. Children (and we were children once) must be taught good boundaries on food, alcohol, sex, and exercise. These boundaries come in the "taught" form of values, personal beliefs, and spiritual beliefs about the use of life's pleasures and activities. It is vital to teach children to say no to destructive behavior that is counterproductive to their own well-being. Did we, as adults, learn these limits? Do we apply these limits in our marriages?

We, as partners in a marriage, need to set our own boundaries within the relationship. Here are some examples:

- How much freedom do you give to the other with regard to being out alone at night and with whom?

- How much time, on the positive side, do we like to spend with each other?

- How much time should be given to work? How much time should each of you put into the family (minimum amount)?

- How much time do you need to spend alone for your own activities?

- What are your expected values on each other for drinking alcohol?

- What are your expected values on drug use, spending of money, helping around the house, and being physically intimate (which includes emotional intimacy)?

There are no "correct" answers to most of these questions. Each person has his or her own view on limits for each of these questions and for other areas not mentioned. The most important point to remember is that because each one of us differs in our responses to boundaries, as a couple, these boundary questions need to be resolved in a marriage, preferably before you are married.

In my work with individuals and with couples, I find that boundary-setting is a must for success in life and for success in a marriage. Without these limits on ourselves and in the marriage, emotional intimacy will not occur at a significant level. Without this boundary level, trust will be questioned and the physical side of intimacy will be challenged.

It is important to do your homework on where you stand in your personal boundaries and where you stand in your agreed-upon couple boundaries.

When a couple sets their boundaries for the marriage, they need to remember to be flexible, other-centered, and clear in their communication of these expectations.

Put a positive twist on boundaries by making them meaningful for your personal growth and meaningful for the personal growth of your marriage.

Boundaries in our personal and marital lives can help us grow intimately closer to those important to us.

QUESTIONS

Boundaries

Do you set limits on
your personal behav-   **ALWAYS** | | | | | **NEVER**
iors?

Do you set limits on
your personal behaviors   **ALWAYS** | | | | | **NEVER**
with the one you love?

Do you set limits on
the behaviors you will   **ALWAYS** | | | | | **NEVER**
accept or limits on the
one you love?

Dynamic Five: Spirituality

Do my beliefs and values really affect my marriage?

"Intimacy is one facet of spirituality. The Latin root *spiritus* means life force, basic energy, being or breath of life, inspiration…intimacy is the inward state involving the deepest relationship with ultimate reality—the self, others, and the environment." (Allen, 2004, p. 15)

"Methods and techniques applied without a permeation or undercoating of grace will quickly lead to chipping, cracking, and eventually peeling. Grace needs to be applied liberally daily within a marriage." (Carlson and Sperry, 1998, p. 426)

Becky and Bruce had been married for eight years when their second child was born physically and mentally challenged. Over the ensuing years, the challenges to both the child and the parents grew. There was not a day without a challenge to the family members who, until recently, handled things the best they could.

Over the last year, however, the parents started to take their frustrations out on each other. Their shortcomings as individuals became targets to attack in each other. There were days when Becky and Bruce wouldn't speak to each other for fear of verbally putting the other down. Their values were challenged, their marriage was at risk, and they were losing their way.

Marriage therapy was chosen by both of them to assist in their efforts to reconnect as a couple. Many topics were discussed, but for both of them, divorce was not an option. Divorce was discussed as a choice, and, in doing so, it brought them to look at their whole value system regarding life, marriage, and family. They realized that they had lost the deeper value of the partner, the family, and their personal lives. This refocusing on the value of the other person as a spiritual being of worth, the refocusing on the family as a reflection of their spiritual values, and the refocusing on themselves as having a spiritual purpose in life helped them look at their marriage with a deeper understanding of their relationship and the deeper meaning of intimacy. This refocusing on their values helped Becky and Bruce give their marriage a stronger commitment to work through troubled times.

I asked a happily married woman of thirty years the question, "How important is spirituality in a relationship?" Her response was directed toward how she felt spirituality affected her:

"Spirituality forms the core of my being. My convictions about what truly matters in this life and how I am to treat others in my relationships flow out of this deeper place in me."

For Laurie, her spirituality gives her guidelines on how to treat others, especially a partner in marriage. Laurie feels she would not have any direction without her spiritual belief system. Life would be chaotic. Life, to her, would be a personally selfish existence without a deeper sense of purpose.

Laurie is confident that a shared spirituality has been one of the key ingredients in the success of her marriage and in the success of her deepest friendships. For her, a shared spirituality invites the other person, as well as herself, to be on the same team, looking together to a higher authority for strength and guidance, rather than making one of them "the boss."

Laurie goes on to state, "Furthermore, rather than asking 'What do I want in this relationship,' my spirituality challenges me daily to ask a far more important question: 'What does my God desire of me?' I believe that God desires that I love others in the same unselfish and forgiving ways in which God himself loves me. If I continually try to keep that faith-based ideal as the standard, I believe this creates an other-centered framework where true love and intimacy can flourish."

Laurie uses her spiritual values to give her some guidelines for loving another person. Being spiritual and having values in a relationship can be helpful for everyone. For many people, being spiritual translates into the religion of their choice. For some, being spiritual means connecting to a higher power in a special way. To others, being spiritual means having good and solid values in life. No matter the different choices, having a spiritual meaning or having values in our lives and relationships adds a needed quality and meaning to them.

When living in a marriage, you must be present! As another person succinctly states, "You need to be present in your relationship to yourself: love yourself; see yourself as a whole person. You must be present in your relationship to your God. You must be present in the relationship to your spouse and family."

Over the years in my work with couples, I have always asked them if spirituality or a strong value system was in play in their marriage. I received a lot of different responses to that question. Many couples responded that they had strong beliefs about marriage; some beliefs were tied to a particular religion, others to family values, and others to personalized beliefs unique to the couple. Some couples had beliefs about marriage, but they got lost when the times got tough. Then there were those who did not have any core beliefs about the values in play for their marriage.

When working within these varied belief systems, I noticed that the couples with the strongest values—religious or personal—had the stronger tenacity required to try and make the marriage work. The values that they lived by helped them deal with the day-to-day challenges of living a coupled life and, for some, a coupled life with children. Values and beliefs fortify our actions to treat the ones we love in a manner that typifies the love and intimacy that they so deserve. Our spirituality, our values challenge us to do better—to be better partners.

The challenge to any couple is to find those beliefs in life that add to our ability to treat our partner in life with dignity, integrity, and intimacy.

Your values and beliefs in life directly affect your ability to be intimate. Talk about them with your significant other.

QUESTIONS

Spirituality (values, religion, belief in a higher power)

Do you know and feel that your spiritual values in life will be accepted by the one you love?

ALWAYS | | | | | NEVER

Do you know and feel you can accept the spiritual values in life that exist in the one you love?

ALWAYS | | | | | NEVER

Are you able to discuss and find compromises on the spiritual values that differ from yours?

ALWAYS | | | | | NEVER

Dynamic Six: Commitment

Am I strong enough to commit forever?

"Commitment…is the aspect that may give relationship meaning to all of the events that take place in marital interaction…Couples have ways of expressing their commitment level that are as individual as they themselves are different as people…Commitment is ever-changing and always elusive." (Stuart, 1981, pp. 99, 100, and 105)

"Intimacy is emotional, involving warmth, connectedness, and feelings of closeness. Passion is a motivational component, including strong desire, often (but not always) sexual, and arousal. Commitment is cognitive; it is a decision to love another person and to secure and maintain a bond with that person." (Reevy, Ozer, and Ito, 2010, p. 330)

Commitment for life is easier to make for some than for others. There have been couples in therapy where one person in the dating relationship has trouble making that final commitment for life to the person they love.

George and Maureen have been dating for six years. Their relationship was going along just fine. They had worked out their minimal differences; they had learned to be flexible when conflicts arose; they were able to consider the other person's viewpoint; they were willing to be open with their feelings; their values were in line with each other; and there was a healthy emotional and physical attraction. The biggest and only significant obstacle was George's reluctance to let go and marry Maureen. There was a block in his mind and in his emotional willingness to give up his individuality, or so he thought.

To simplify what happened with George, he did finally understand that his fear of completely committing to Maureen involved fear of rejection, which turned out to be an unfounded fear from the past. The basis of his fear of being rejected was not by Maureen, but a fear that was still rooted in a past relationship with another woman and a fear that had some basis in his mother's non-acceptance of the women he chose. As George told me, his mother would say, "There is no woman good enough for you. They will trick you into believing they love you and then take all your money and leave you." George didn't believe this, but it greatly influenced his unwillingness to commit. The short ending is that George and Maureen together overcame his fear of her rejecting him. Ten years later, I still see them in town, and they never fail to mention to me how happy they are to be together. To watch them together, you know it is true. Neither doubts they are committed to the other.

Commitment to anything that is long-term takes character, determination, and strength. Unfortunately, we do not get a lot of practice in making long-term or life-long commitments, as most commitments are short in duration, not difficult, or require no choice. Some examples might be:

- We expect to sleep every day and drink and eat something each day. For almost everyone, these behaviors are not difficult to do for the average person and thus, do not involve much of a commitment.

- It requires very little choice to commit to paying our taxes or paying our bills, as we do not like the consequences of not paying them.

- Losing five pounds of body weight is a commitment, but requires a limited amount of effort and, once reached, we no longer have the same goal; this particular commitment is over. Keeping it off is a different goal. (Yes, you can argue that losing five pounds may take you a lifetime. Sorry, that doesn't count.)

There is also the difference between our personal goals or commitments and commitments to another person. The commitment for life to our partner is a deeper commitment, one that requires more effort and determination. When we involve two people in a commitment, we have to be aware of our effect on others as we carry out our end of the agreement. When we personally commit ourselves to do something, we affect only one person if we fail or choose not to follow through. It is easier to change what, when, or how we want to do something for ourselves than it is to make changes if someone else is involved.

Just imagine how your life would be different if you were not committed to someone. There would be changes in how you live your life. I'm not saying you want these changes, but by being committed to someone, it does alter your life (hopefully, for the better). It usually makes your life more meaningful. Sharing your life with someone does have great advantages, and they are better when you know you can count on these advantages by being able to count on the person being there with you.

There are certain things that are important to remember when you commit to someone for life:

- Commitment is a choice. You are choosing to be with that person. No one should be forcing you to do so. Commitments that do not involve your willingness have their own concerns and issues.

- When you commit to someone, do not do so hoping the person will change after you marry. You must be able to accept them as they now present themselves to you. A person who gets drunk too often may continue to drink even more after you are married. A person who has "cheated" on you twice after you both had agreed to not see anyone else may continue that "roving" after you are married. Someone who has a serious lack of control with his or her anger will probably continue to do so after he or she is married, unless control is learned before marriage. A person who continually spends beyond his or her means will continue to do so, unless control is learned before marriage. *What you see before you marry is probably what you will get after you are married.*

- Commitment should be taken seriously by both parties. Make sure you and the person you will be marrying agree upon each other's definition of commitment.

- Look for values, behaviors, and feelings that could possibly challenge your commitment to the other person. Do you agree on having children or not having children? This is an important decision. Do you agree on how you will parent your children should you choose to have them? Do you agree on your abilities to be emotionally, spiritually, and physically intimate at a level that is satisfying to both of you? Could the course of your careers affect your level of commitment? Are there any past, unresolved issues that could get in the way of the marriage?

- Ask yourself if you are emotionally ready to commit to anything for a lifetime. Have you matured enough? Do you need to "grow up" and be a more responsible and other-centered person before you commit to someone else?

- Do you feel right in your "gut" or in your instincts about the other person or even about your own decision to marry? If no, please check out these feelings with a professional.

- Being able to commit is a vital ingredient in a lasting marriage. Commitment provides a secure base for one partner to be vulnerable to the other person and to put trust in that person. I will get into these two dynamics next.

- Anyone would be foolish to enter into any contract without a solid commitment on both sides.

- Commitments will be challenged, just as loving someone during difficult moments is challenging. During these times of challenge, you pull on the values of commitment to provide an impetus to find solutions to the present challenges. Commitment is part of the glue that keeps you together as you grow in your abilities to work out difficulties.

- *Commitment should mean that you will never take each other for granted.*

Generally, the biggest commitment that I feel needs to be a focus in our lives—other than a spiritual commitment—is our commitment to the one we love. When we commit to someone to love them for life, are we capable of doing this? Are we willing to do so when the going gets tough? This is where our values and spiritual beliefs about commitment give us strength to work it out. If we do not think we can commit to loving someone for life, then we need to be honest and tell them so before we say "I do." Many of the other dynamics mentioned in this book can add to our ability to stay committed. If we are flexible, trustworthy, other-centered, vulnerable, and spiritual, plus have boundaries and are able to forgive, then all of these add to our ability to stay committed.

If we are able and willing to stay committed in our significant relationship (marriage), this ability can help us stay committed in other areas of our life, such as the unconditional love of our children, a commitment to a special friend, a commitment to our spiritual beliefs, and a commitment to providing excellent work in our job or career. These and other commitments are all a part of who we are as people who possess the ability to follow through and stay with the promises that we make in life.

Remember, it takes two to commit. It takes only one to destroy a commitment.

Commitment is an ability that should be highly valued.

QUESTIONS

Commitment

Are you willing to
commit to the one you
love for life, which   **ALWAYS** | | | | | **NEVER**
includes working
through difficulties?

Is the one you love
willing to commit
to you for life, which   **ALWAYS** | | | | | **NEVER**
includes working
through difficulties?

Are you willing to
openly discuss any
"deal-breaker" issues   **ALWAYS** | | | | | **NEVER**
that could make com-
mitment more diffi-
cult?

Is your partner willing
to openly discuss any
"deal-breaker" issues   ALWAYS | | | | | NEVER
that could make com-
mitment more diffi-
cult?

Part Three

This section focuses on an advanced understanding of the self and a willingness of the self to be emotionally involved with someone else.

> **Dynamic Seven: Vulnerability**
>
> **Dynamic Eight: Trust**
>
> **Dynamic Nine: Forgiveness**

Dynamic Seven: Vulnerability

Am I willing to be emotionally open with anyone?

"When you hide from, deny, avoid, and run away from your vulnerability in the world then you stunt your personal and spiritual growth. It is only by authentically showing up without all the self-protective stories and habits accumulated over a lifetime that we are able to

truly be intimate with our lives and with our partners."
(Cordova, 2009, p. 137)

"In an intimate relationship, vulnerability is a state of existence." (Linder, 2006, p. 16)

Melody and James married when they were both twenty-one years old. Three years later, Melody sought out marital therapy for both of them, stating that they were having serious problems in communicating, trusting, and feeling intimate with each other. Reluctantly, James came with Melody to "try" counseling.

In partner or marital therapy, it is important to find the "root" causes to the difficulty each couple may be experiencing in their unique relationship. No two partnerships are the same. Each has its own twists, history, and problems. Aside from poor communication and listening styles and a history of multiple parental divorces on both sides, Melody and James, with the help of therapy, determined that both of them had a history of not trusting that the other person was truly committed to them. Prior to James, Melody had been "in love" with two other men; both of them cheated on her. Melody stated that she never felt emotionally close to either parent, but especially not to her father, who was never home, was an alcoholic, and left the family when Melody was ten years old. James came from a family hit by divorce. His mother left James's dad when James was six. His dad remarried a year later, only to divorce nine months later. James's mother had also married, divorced, and married her third husband. Emotions of love and caring were shown minimally toward James and his sister. James had had a lot of short-term relationships before Melody.

Both James and Melody stated that they never really trusted in any relationship and doubted if either one was open to letting the other into his/her life and emotional space. Neither one felt that he/she had been emotionally intimate with the other. The closest form of mutual intimacy was physical intimacy, and this was rapidly decreasing due to the lack of ability to communicate and trust each other. Neither was able to open up and be vulnerable enough to trust and let the other person into his or her heart.

Vulnerability is the quality needed in a person that lets him or her trust another person. To be vulnerable in a relationship does not mean that we trust the other person immediately. We build upon our willingness to be open to loving deeply. This involves our risking reaching out and caring for a person with no guarantee that this reaching out and opening up will be equally reciprocated. We, in doing this, risk being hurt and rejected. But the risk is qualified before we reach out.

This reaching out—this being open to someone to form a closer relationship—is a selective process. We can be open to loving people in general, but to be open to being in a special loving relationship with someone is a unique process.

What does it mean to be open, to be vulnerable? Here are some thoughts on this process.

- To be open to being loved by that special person, a person needs to have worked out any past negative life experiences that may have shut down his/her willingness to be open to a significant relationship.

- Lack of parental emotional bonding may negatively influence our future willingness to be open.

- Lack of parental emotional bonding may have not given us the knowledge and feelings we need to be able to be vulnerable to someone's genuine love.

- Without early emotional bonding experiences in our lives, we may not even know we are missing out on something that is an integral part of our being emotionally close to someone.

- We may not realize that past negative experiences such as physical abuse, sexual abuse, emotional rejection, and verbal abuse may have altered our willingness to be vulnerable to someone loving us.

- We need to remember that being vulnerable to someone does not mean that we are not self-protective. It does not mean that we completely let our guard down.

- Being vulnerable can mean that we have freed ourselves from anything that might block our attempts to be open. (I am referring to serious blocks from the past.)

- Being vulnerable with that special person takes time. It is a slow process.

- Being vulnerable to someone special must feel good to us, and this feeling continues to grow with time.

- Not only must being vulnerable feel good, but also it must intellectually and spiritually be a wise and healthy decision to be involved with this person.

- We need to be confident in ourselves. We need to want to be open and share our thoughts and feelings with someone. We need to feel confident enough in ourselves, that we are coming from a good place in our hearts; that if our openness to get close to someone is rejected, we will feel it is their loss...their loss in that they could not see in us the truth in our intentions to want to reach out to them with good feelings.

Being vulnerable means reaching out to someone you have carefully chosen to make a connection with and then trying to understand his or her wants and who he or she is, while revealing some of who you are and what you stand for.

Being vulnerable emotionally is generally a close partner to being physically intimate. This physical intimacy is able to grow because of the willingness of both partners to be open to expressing emotional intimacy.

These thoughts on vulnerability came from a very happily married woman who had strong feelings on this topic. She states, "I feel vulnerability is a requirement if I am going to be intimately connected with another person. The vulnerability also goes two ways—my partner must also be willing to be vulnerable with me.

"Vulnerability means removing protective walls so that you get to know and understand the real me and that includes all dimensions of me: my wants, my needs, my beliefs, my values, my dreams, my passions, my fears, and my faults and failures.

"I have to love myself completely and appropriately, so that I am emotionally strong enough to handle the risk required to fully expose myself to another person.

"Being vulnerable involves healthy risk and definitely takes courage. And if I do make myself vulnerable and find I am rejected, as long as I have a clear awareness of my own identity and plenty of self-love, I will survive and heal. Eventually, I will be able to put the real me out there again and, hopefully, this time someone new will be willing to accept the imperfect yet still beautiful me.

"Yes, loving—really loving—always involves taking a chance, but the sweetness of intimacy is oh-so worth the risk."

Some other general thoughts on vulnerability should, in my opinion, include the fact that even though we may have been emotionally hurt in the past by someone important to us, most people who try can override those past feelings of rejection and learn how to be open to a meaningful relationship.

The deeper the hurt in the past, the longer it could take to become emotionally open to another person. I have had the opportunity to help many over the years move beyond their negative past experiences and become more willing to risk loving and caring for someone else and letting someone else be loving and caring to them. This moving on and making yourself vulnerable is a very personal and unique event for those who have been hurt. The circumstances, the people involved, the duration, and the intensity of the negative experience all affect the recovery process. As my clients of all ages and both sexes have told me, the effort needed to move to a better place emotionally, spiritually, physically, and intellectually was worth it. Their lives have changed for the better.

As we gain a loving sense of self and feel good about our ability to love someone else, this will make risking our love a lot easier. Be confident in yourself before you love anyone else.

There comes a sense of peace within us as we comfortably reach out and are open to someone else who shares the same level of openness and vulnerability. This sense of peace with our partner—this sense of openness—needs to be present and kept alive in your relationship. We need to talk out our differences, our fears, and our wanting to close up our vulnerability.

Vulnerability is present in other parts of our lives to a differing degree. It is usually involved in our very special relationships. These relationships can include your God (higher power), your family of origin, your children, and your significant other. Being open to loving them and being loved by them is important. This openness will make those relationships more meaningful. Only you will know if you are closed off in some way in any of those relationships.

Another point: there are some people who are not aware that they are blocked, not willing to be open to emotional intimacy. They have never experienced this vulnerability with anyone. They will get involved in a relationship and feel close to someone, usually physically (as in sexually), but over time, this physical attraction dies and they often hear from their partners that they do not feel close to them anymore. The emotional intimacy is missing. The emotional vulnerability probably has never been there in the partner who had never experienced this openness in her/his life. It is time to ask for help.

Couples should become aware of the times they close off to their partners—times when they feel emotionally distant and don't want to be open to any form of closeness. When these times happen, the two of you need to take the time to sit down and talk out what is happening between you. Use your communication skills, be other-centered, be flexible, and listen well to each other, as you resolve the feelings of being closed off to the other. Again, seek help if you can't resolve the issues on your own, but do not let this closed-off feeling continue for any length of time. The longer the distance between you continues, the stronger the negative feelings become.

To be able to be open to the person you love is a very freeing experience, well worth the risk and effort.

QUESTIONS

Vulnerability

Are you willing to
let yourself feel the
positive emotion being   **ALWAYS** | | | | | **NEVER**
shared with you by the
one you love?

Are you willing to
openly show your feel-
ings to the one you   **ALWAYS** | | | | | **NEVER**
love?

Are you willing to risk
being emotionally hurt   **ALWAYS** | | | | | **NEVER**
by the one you love?

Dynamic Eight:
Trust

Am I trustworthy?

"A trusting partner believes that she or he faces little risk of harm, exploitation, betrayal, or deceit from another as a result of any intimate encounter the two partners may have." (Gurtman, 1992, p. 992)

"Since intimacy involves revealing the vulnerable parts of the self, partners must trust one another to continue to interact intimately, almost by definition." (Prager, 1998, p. 25)

Mike and Jenny had been married thirteen years before recognizable trouble hit their marriage. Mike is an attractive male with high community acceptance. Jenny is a strikingly beautiful woman who also has great community acceptance. They have three children together, all in the lower grades in school. Both Mike and Jenny are in top management positions in their respective jobs, and both work long hours and are involved in some travel for their work. All seemed to be going well in the marriage until Jenny found, by accident, some voice messages on Mike's cell phone from another woman. Jenny had never been concerned that Mike would get involved with someone else, so she had never checked his cell phone before. But these messages were about Mike's meeting a woman to discuss "business" on a Thursday evening when Jenny was out of town. A warning flag went up in Jenny's mind. She figured she needed to talk to Mike about this, and she did. Mike said the woman was from work, and she had not been aware when she asked to get together that Jenny would be out of town. Mike told the woman that she needed to come to his office to discuss the "business" topic.

Several months went by. Jenny would quietly spot-check Mike's cell phone but found nothing. She did notice that he was becoming more distant and seemed to not be paying as much attention to her. Then, out of the blue, Jenny got a phone call from one of Mike's coworkers, telling her that Mike seemed to be paying too much attention to a woman at work, and people were starting to notice seeing them quite often in public together during the lunch hour. The coworker was giving Jenny a heads-up. Jenny became concerned again, as the woman in question was the same person who had called Mike on his cell phone.

She again confronted Mike about the phone call and the attention he was giving this woman. She also mentioned she was feeling a growing lack of interest in her. Mike denied anything was going on and said he would try to give Jenny more attention.

Rather than just let this matter be, Jenny made an appointment for both of them with a therapist. Mike reluctantly agreed to go, but he admitted to Jenny that there was a distance growing between them. Therapy started with the goal of becoming closer emotionally and for Jenny, a goal of processing her concerns about the woman at work. In the therapy process, it can take time for people to open up to their deeper feelings. Trust in the therapy process, trust in one's self to be willing to be open, trust in the therapist to be able to help them, and trust in the other person's willingness to be open had to be established. Fortunately, as the therapist, I was able to help them see that things between them would not get better unless they were completely honest with each other.

In time, the therapy process allowed them to talk about some of the "unspoken" problems in their relationship. The "never discussed reasons" for Mike's pulling away from Jenny. His concerns about the marriage finally came to the surface and were openly examined and explained. Mike admitted that he was involved with this woman at work, but it had not developed, in Mike's opinion, into a sexual relationship and therefore, it had not gone too far.

For Jenny, any emotional relationship outside the marriage was breaking the trust between the two of them. Mike, in the past, had not been honest about his feelings for the other woman and had not been honest about his growing lack of feelings for Jenny. Mike did not trust in himself and in Jenny to talk to her about his feelings. He also broke the trust by turning to another woman to share his emotional self, as he emotionally pulled away from Jenny.

The two worked on their issues together in therapy. The biggest issue for Jenny was being able to trust that Mike truly loved her and that he could openly talk to her if he had a problem. The trust issue was a catalyst to get into other issues of concern to them. They grew to trust that each truly wanted the relationship to work. They were open to finding ways to handle problems as they arose and not bottle them up and react to them by turning to someone else for support. Learning to trust that they both would be open with their feelings and not let issues bottle up became a major step in their drawing emotionally closer to each other.

Trust is so vital in all areas of our life. It extends from trust in yourself, to family, to your marriage partner, to your coworkers, to your country. I met and listened to Stephen M. R. Covey as he so brilliantly discussed trust in his book, *The Speed of Trust*, a must-read for all of us. Trust deeply affects each one of us in some way.

Stephen Covey starts his first chapter with this statement: "There is one thing that is common to every individual, relationship, team, family, organization, nation, economy, and civilization throughout the world—one thing which, if removed, will destroy the most powerful government, the most successful business, the most thriving economy, the most influential leadership, the greatest friendship, the strongest character, the deepest love.

"On the other hand, if developed and leveraged, that one thing has the potential to create unparalleled success and prosperity in every dimension of life. Yet it is the least understood, most neglected, and most underestimated possibility of our time.

"That one thing is trust.

"Contrary to what most people believe, trust is not some soft, illusive quality that you either have or you don't; rather, trust is a pragmatic, tangible, actionable asset that you can create— much faster than you probably think possible."

Later in this chapter, I will briefly mention Stephen Covey's thirteen behaviors that he states will significantly enhance one's ability to establish trust in all relationships, both personal and professional. These thirteen behaviors can be tailored into trust in a relationship.

I find trust to be a major factor in the lasting success of a relationship. But first, you must ask yourself if you are trustworthy. Do you live up to your personal values? Can the person in your life count on you to tell the truth, that lying is never acceptable? Can you own up to your behaviors in life and be honest with your marriage partner? This is a dynamic that reaches into the core of your values.

Trust, like most of the other dynamics, begins early in life. We learn to be honest from our parents. We are taught to tell the truth. We were taught the principle of honesty, which allows for trust to occur. Trust in our parents is often unconsciously tested by us growing up. When we first cried as a baby and a parent responded, we began being able to trust. When we hurt ourselves, when our parents caught us in a lie, when we failed our first exam, when we lost our first game, and when we were scared, our parents were there to comfort us and remind us that they loved us. Those were trust-building moments. Even when our parents had to tell us "no," when they had to ground us, send us to our room, or when they had to "talk" to us about our behavior, these were also trust-building moments, even though at the time we may not have understood the positive impact of these events. Trust was built by knowing, later in life, our parents loved us enough to set boundaries to teach us how to effectively and appropriately live life. If only we, when we were younger, could have realized that our parents were trying to help us. Unfortunately, not all parents know how to teach trust, as a lot of their own actions do not build trust in others. They, as children, did not learn to trust in others.

Once we have learned the meaning of trust from our parents, we begin to cautiously trust others in our life—our classmates, our neighbors, our after-school friends. While we are growing up, our parents try to help us decide who is trustworthy and who we should watch out for as friends. We may not have always been in agreement with our parents, but we learned how to discern what trust in a friend should mean.

As we grow and learn about trust in other people, we ultimately—if we choose—will face the true test of trusting someone in a love relationship. Trusting the one we take on as a lifelong partner is a true challenge and a vital ingredient in a committed relationship. Each one of us in a committed relationship has thought of what is needed from the other to feel that we can trust him/her—what is needed to feel that he/she will not do something that would break our heart and destroy the relationship.

What are the deal-breakers in a relationship? What would challenge the trust of the other person enough for him/her to call off the relationship? The answers to these questions vary with the uniqueness of each couple and vary with the stage the couples are in. Are they recently engaged, married for one year, or married as long as fifty years? No matter. The couples need to openly communicate the "deal-breakers" for their particular relationship.

To build trust, both people in the relationship must understand that there are certain boundaries that, if broken, would be cause for the relationship to end. When those boundaries are established and committed to, the path to trusting is started. It doesn't mean that trust is now guaranteed, but at least both agree not to violate these boundaries.

What helps a couple maintain trust or build trust in a relationship?

- Be honest. Never lie to your partner.

- If your partner offends you or doesn't understand your feelings, talk about it before it becomes a big issue.

- Never go to bed angry. Agree to settle the issue the next day.

- Find resolutions to differences even if you have to ask for outside help, like a therapist or another person you both trust.

- Talk about each of your areas of sensitivity—areas where you can easily be hurt and may lead you to not trust the other person. For example, if someone cheated on you in the past with a coworker, your weakness or sensitivity may be around your partner spending too much time socializing with coworkers after work. Talk about these sensitive areas and come to a resolution or compromise solution.

- When concerns arise, be open and flexible in discussing them.

- Choose friends and other couples who are trustworthy.

- If you feel you cannot trust the person in your life, please get help.

If all people made themselves trustworthy, the world would be a much better place. Creating trust must start with you and reach out to all those around you. Take your trust, and teach others to trust.

Let's look at the thirteen behaviors of Stephen M. R. Covey, which will help us increase trust in our lives. To get the full meaning of these behaviors, you will need to read his book, *The Speed of Trust*. I hope these behaviors will engage you and inspire you to deepen your level of trust.

1. <u>Talk Straight</u> – Be honest. Let people know where you stand. Demonstrate integrity. Don't manipulate people or distort facts.

2. <u>Demonstrate Respect</u> – Genuinely care for others. Show you care. Respect the dignity of every person and every role. Show kindness in the little things. Don't fake caring.

3. <u>Create Transparency</u> – Tell the truth in a way people can verify. Be open and authentic. Err on the side of disclosure. Don't hide information.

4. <u>Right Wrongs</u> – Make things right when you're wrong. Apologize quickly. Demonstrate humility. Don't let personal pride get in the way of doing the right thing.

5. <u>Show Loyalty</u> – Give credit to others. Speak about people as if they were present. Don't badmouth others behind their backs. Don't disclose others' private information.

6. <u>Deliver Results</u> – Establish a track record of results. Get the right things done. Don't overpromise and under-deliver. Do not make excuses for not delivering.

7. <u>Get Better</u> – Continuously improve. Be a constant learner. Develop feedback systems, both formal and informal. Don't consider yourself above feedback.

8. <u>Confront Reality</u> – Take issues head on, even the "undiscussables." Address the tough stuff directly. Confront the reality, not the person.

9. <u>Clarify Expectations</u> – Disclose and reveal expectations. Discuss them. Validate them. Renegotiate them if needed and possible. Don't assume that expectations are clear or shared.

10. <u>Practice Accountability</u> – Hold yourself accountable. Hold others accountable. Don't avoid or shirk responsibility. Don't blame others or point fingers when things go wrong.

11. <u>Listen First</u> – Listen before you speak. Don't assume you know what matters most to others. Don't presume you have all the answers—or all the questions.

12. <u>Keep Commitments</u> – Say what you are going to do. Then do what you say you're going to do. Make

commitments carefully, and keep them at all costs. Make keeping commitments the symbol of your honor.

13. Extend Trust – Demonstrate a propensity to trust. Extend trust abundantly to those who have earned your trust. Learn how to appropriately extend trust to others based on the situation, risk, and credibility of the people involved.

All thirteen behaviors listed in Stephen M. R. Covey's book *The Speed of Trust* can be used in the marriage setting. Without these behaviors, experiencing trust will be more difficult. Without trust, you have no marriage.

When trust has been broken, you must move on but never give up. A former client has written her thoughts on trust to share with us. Here's what she had to say:

"Trust is loyalty, safety, and reliance, a word that describes the confidence to depend on one another as well as the hope for a future with this person you 'trust.' Trust is an important element for a successful marriage.

"It is frustrating that I am good at allowing men who are not trustworthy to choose me as a significant other, yet I choose amazingly honest and dependable girlfriends. I have briefly endured two marriages, both which were to men who adored me, would do anything for me, and pursued me as I was independent and not highly interested in marriage… As each of them eventually won my heart, I happily agreed to take marriage vows. For each, the hunt was over soon after the marriage vows were exchanged, and each of them quietly moved on to new prey, thus the end of each marriage.

"It is icing on the cake to have a significant other as a rock—meaning if the significant other is not trustworthy, one is better off alone. I do envy those who have a significant other who is trustworthy. Before my second marriage, we discussed that either my husband was going to be the man of honor that I deserved or he was not, and I would be okay with being on my own once again. Within a month of that wonderful feel-good conversation (of trust in each other), my husband's phone dinged with a text from another woman. I took his phone to him, and he denied it. It is amazing the detective a wife can become with no training. It was true. Granted it was just the beginning; however, he had initiated and was continuing an extensive secret emotional affair with another woman. I left him.

"To have a trusting significant other and the ability to trust oneself are two separate and important aspects in a relationship. We are all human. We do and will make mistakes. Mistakes are human and acceptable, when not purposefully deceitful and routinely hurtful to family, friends, or strangers. To put forth effort to learn from one's mistakes to reduce the likelihood of repeating them is an indispensable life lesson. Trust of oneself and one's significant other is vital, as trust is a cornerstone for a healthy relationship and marriage."

The ending to this woman's story of her two significant relationships was good for her. She has become very self-reliant and content with her currently single lifestyle. She has not lost hope that she will someday find a man she is willing to trust and who is willing to trust her. She feels she has grown from these experiences and will not let them negatively affect the rest of her life. For her, trust will be possible in the next relationship, a relationship that is not a must or need, but a want in her life.

To be a trustworthy person is to be a person of honorable character.

QUESTIONS

Trust

Are you honest and
truthful when you
communicate with the
one you love?

ALWAYS | | | | | **NEVER**

Is the one you love
always honest and
truthful with you?

ALWAYS | | | | | **NEVER**

Do you both agree
on the importance of
being able to trust each
other in all of the areas
in your lives together?

ALWAYS | | | | | **NEVER**

Dynamic Nine: Forgiveness

Is forgiveness in my heart?

"Before one can share hurts and fears of being hurt, forgiveness needs to be included. Otherwise, it is difficult, if not impossible, to achieve intimacy." (L'Abate, 2005, p. 349)

"The benefits of forgiving for individual well-being have been documented across a variety of domains, including physical health, mental health, and life satisfaction. Given the association between individual and relationship health, this raises the question of whether forgiveness might not have similarly beneficial implications for close relationships such as marriage." (Fincham and Beach, 2007, p. 260)

Once you have been emotionally hurt deeply, it can take a while to recover. However, before you can recover, it may be necessary to forgive the person or people involved.

There are many situations in life where the hurt from someone else's behavior can affect our trust in him/her:

- Lies/dishonesty: big and little, depending on frequency and how significant the meaning of the lie is to the person offended.

- Verbal abuse, which is also dependent on what is said, how it is said, how often it happens, and the intensity of the delivery. If it offends the person you are talking to, ask yourself if it could be abusive. Better yet, ask the person who was subjected to your words.

- Physical abuse is easier to recognize. If you touch or hit anyone in anger, it will probably be physically abusive. We can't let ourselves hit anyone, nor allow ourselves to be hit by anyone. This is a general rule. I am not talking about self-defense.

- Sexual abuse can easily destroy trust and have many other negative effects on the person abused.

- Infidelity.

- When the self is always more important than anyone else.

There are many related categories to the above-named abuses. There are specific abuses to specific people and specific situations. It is not my purpose to identify all the ways in which a person can be abused, nor can I identify all the ways trust can be lost between two people or groups of people. What I would like us to do is to become aware of how we might hurt others by our words or actions and become aware of our ability to negatively affect those around us.

Also, be aware of how others may hurt you or have hurt you and your willingness to forgive them. Whether you hurt others or others have hurt you, forgiveness—when safe to do so—may be part of your path to personal recovery and growth.

In marriage therapy, I have run into many couples where one of the partners has abused the other in some fashion. An increasingly common reason for couples to seek marital therapy involves infidelity: One of the partners cheated on the other. They are coming to therapy to determine if they can get past the infidelity and move to a better and stronger place in their marriage.

Rachel and Brad had been married for eight years. They have two children together, ages five and seven. They both work full time. She is a teacher, and he is a marketer for a large firm and is required to travel out of town an average of three nights a week. Rachel doesn't like this situation, but Brad's job pays well and the potential to move up in the company is great. Both come from divorced homes and from families where discord was common. Before they got married, both Rachel and Brad promised each other that their marriage was going to be different from the marriages of their parents.

Having two children who demanded a lot of attention, two demanding jobs, and little time for the two of them to be together was causing significant stress between them. They had never learned how to communicate effectively, how to listen to each other, or how to resolve conflicts effectively. They had never made the time to work on these issues.

A distance was growing between them. Brad was finding himself pulling away from Rachel but not telling her how he was feeling. Rachel, as a teacher who always had work to do in preparation for the next school day, let her concerns for the marriage slide. Being gone as many as three nights a week gave Brad a lot of time to think. He started to feel sorry for himself and lonely. As they grew apart, so did their physical intimacy. Without trying to make the marriage better, Brad let himself become attracted to one of his marketing contacts away from home. She was in the process of getting divorced. The time was ripe for a relationship between them. Their communication about their mutual marital problems turned into (at first) an emotional closeness with no boundaries to a physical expression of this newly found closeness.

Rachel found out about Brad's relationship with this woman. She had a choice: she could work on the issues in the marriage, or she could tell Brad he had broken the trust she had in him in such an impactful way that she felt she could never forgive him and trust him again. Brad had to decide if he could be worthy of her trust and give Rachel the love she deserves. They both had decisions to make about their future.

They both willingly came to therapy. One of my requirements for anyone in couple's therapy is that both must be willing to try to make the relationship a meaningful and loving experience for both of them. Both must be willing to make changes for the betterment of the relationship. If one or both of them are not willing to work on the relationship, then individual therapy is necessary until one or both decides against trying to help the marriage, or both agree to try couple's therapy.

Rachel and Brad worked hard in couple's therapy. They identified why they wanted to stay together. They looked at the causes and solutions to their marital issues. Rachel worked through her hurt and disappointment and anger at Brad for breaking their trust with an affair. Conditions were met that allowed Rachel to begin the forgiveness part of the process. Also, Rachel realized that she, too, was involved in the marriage falling apart. An affair is never justified, but Rachel—with Brad's sincere input—learned that both of them needed to grow in becoming more emotionally intimate, a process that was often neglected in their marriage. Also, they learned new ways of being emotionally intimate, which led them to better physical intimacy. There were strong-enough, original emotional connections that allowed Rachel to process forgiveness and allow herself to "grow" trust again—maybe even to a deeper level than before. Brad realized that he had not been honest about his diminishing feelings for Rachel. Brad took action without ever trying to get help for the two of them. Brad needed to forgive himself for acting on his feelings for another woman without even considering trying to make their marriage work. Brad also needed to be sincere in asking Rachel for forgiveness for his affair. He should be aware that this might take time.

The ending to this story was the ending both of them realized they wanted. They worked hard on making the changes they needed in order for them to grow into the emotional intimacy they both longed for. The energy, time, and willingness were worth it. They achieved their goal.

When events happen in our lives that warrant forgiveness, are we willing to ask for forgiveness? Can you forgive yourself for what you might have done to others?

You probably won't go through life without hurting someone, whether you intend to or not. You probably won't go through life without being hurt by someone, intentionally or not. So forgiveness should be a consideration in life, especially in a marriage.

Forgiveness can have many layers of depth. Forgiving someone for forgetting your birthday is not the same as forgiving someone who had an affair while committed to you. There are many factors that come into play when considering whether or not to forgive a person. Some of these factors might include:

1. Was the transgression intentional or by accident?

2. Was it an oft-repeated transgression with no intention of trying to stop?

3. How emotionally close was the person who offended you? Was it a sibling, parent, child, partner, spouse, coworker, friend, acquaintance, stranger, or someone else not mentioned?

4. The nature of the transgression is also significant. Was it a small lie, big lie, or an unforgettable offense?

5. Are there many other unique factors involved in your situation that might alter your willingness to forgive?

As a psychologist, I see many people who have been significantly hurt by someone important to them or important to their future. The one common theme of those who have been deeply offended is realizing how difficult it is to move on emotionally after having been hurt. Many emotions arise when recalling the event or events that happened to them. Some experience fear; some experience anger, rejection, hatred, revenge, and a host of other feelings. It is important to be aware of these feelings.

I mention forgiveness as a quality in life that can be important to possess. In my experience with clients who have been deeply offended, those who are able to make efforts to appropriately move on come out feeling better about themselves and their lives. Those who are not able to move on seem to be in an emotionally ineffective place in life. In either situation, I am not trying to minimize the damage done to the people who have been hurt. The experience can be very emotionally devastating. Therapy is important for people going through this hurt.

In a marriage, staying angry or hurt will make moving on impossible until some type of resolution is achieved. Anger will understandably make you emotionally unavailable to the one you love. This self-protection will remain until you are able to move on.

There are people who do not want to try to forgive and move on in life, but holding onto this anger or any strong negative feeling toward anyone will only eat away at your emotional and physical well-being. The appropriate "letting go" of what happened to you—this forgiveness process—can be very rewarding emotionally and physically.

I used the example of Rachel and Brad as an illustration of a marriage issue, an infidelity that would need forgiveness before the couple could move on in repairing the relationship. It is difficult, to say the least, to forgive infidelity. In any marriage, both parties must want to save the relationship. The best chance of forgiving and moving on after any trust-breaking event will depend, like it did for Rachel and Brad, on the depth of "glue" the marriage has from its start. When marriages possess, to a significant degree, the qualities of other-centeredness, flexibility, vulnerability, good communication, trust, spirituality, and the ability to love, the chances are greater for the couple to resolve the reasons for the infidelity and move on together. Nestled in these qualities is the ability to forgive.

An affair is a negatively powerful wake-up call to refocus on the importance of why the two of you are together, what went wrong, and what needs to be done to never let this happen again. It will take time to feel that the other person can be trusted. It takes courage to want to reassess the quality of love between the two of you. It takes courage, common sense, intelligent decision-making, emotional willingness to be vulnerable again, and great communication skills to forgive and begin to move on.

Forgiveness frees the soul and spirit to move on. Forgiveness can be healing.

Becoming emotionally healthy as an individual allows a person the strength to appropriately forgive.

QUESTIONS

Forgiveness

Are you able to talk through and resolve the feelings of being hurt by the one you love?

ALWAYS | | | | | **NEVER**

Are you generally able to forgive someone who has hurt you, but who is sincerely sorry and makes genuine efforts to never hurt you in that way again?

ALWAYS | | | | | **NEVER**

Is the one you love able
to forgive you if you
have hurt him/her, but
you are sincerely sorry   ALWAYS | | | | | NEVER
and make genuine
efforts to never hurt
him/her in that way
again?

Are you willing to for-
give when appropriate   ALWAYS | | | | | NEVER
and move on from past
hurtful events?

Is the one you love
willing to forgive when
appropriate and move   ALWAYS | | | | | NEVER
on from past hurtful
events?

Part Four

This section focuses on achieving the goal. The goal is to be emotionally, physically, and spiritually fulfilled in ways that culminate in a committed love.

Committed Love and Better Physical Intimacy

Committed Love and Better Physical Intimacy

Do I feel the internal beauty in the person I love?

"Consummate love results from the combinations of all three components: intimacy, passion, and a commitment to the relationship." (Prilleltensky and Prilleltensky, 2006, p. 131)

"Mature love is a complex combination of sexual excitement, tenderness, commitment, and—most of all—an overriding passion that sets it apart from all other love relationships in one's life. The passion isn't simply a matter of orgasm but also entails a crossing of the psychological boundaries between oneself and one's lover. You feel as if you're becoming one with your partner while simultaneously retaining a sense of yourself." (Hales, 2008, p. 247)

A twenty-three-year-old male came to me for therapy because he was anxious and worried that he was losing his sexual ability to perform with his new girlfriend. The first time they tried to "have sex," he could not get nor maintain an erection. They tried being physically intimate many times but to no avail. He left the girl he was dating and then decided to get help. He— let's call him Darren—eventually went to a medical doctor and underwent a complete physical, including a check of his testosterone levels. All were good. There was not a physical issue. Darren then decided to come see me.

A complete psychological history was taken on Darren, including his dating and sexual experiences in the past. It turns out Darren had never been happy with his looks. He felt fat. He had been brought up with the strong belief that you waited to have sex until you were married. He doesn't believe this now, but feels his past belief about having sexual relations before marriage may still be influencing him. The longest relationship he ever had lasted two months when he was fifteen years old. Since he was fourteen, he has been into porn. Darren would get into a relationship and, within a date or two, try to have sexual intercourse. He was not able to maintain an erection long enough to ejaculate when he was with a woman. He states he has a performance anxiety that he cannot seem to overcome.

We discussed a lot in therapy. Darren was able to talk about his lack of self-confidence that occurs whenever he is dating a woman. He talked about being self-conscious about a woman seeing him naked. He explained that he broke his lovemaking into parts; the whole process is preprogramed in his mind. His entire focus is on how well he is doing in the lovemaking process. While making love, he grades himself on his performance. Was he good enough for the woman?

This young man's story has been simplified and many details have been left out that would be important to know in therapy, but they are not important to the point I want to make about Darren's success in overcoming his problem. Darren discussed his religious beliefs, his beliefs about believing in himself, and his beliefs about being sexually intimate and emotionally intimate with the woman he is dating. During one of the sessions, we had an intense discussion on his willingness to trust a woman enough to be able to openly feel an emotional response to her and appreciate who she is as a person without thinking of how he was going to "perform" in bed with her. Darren responded to the discussion by stating that during his lovemaking he did not focus on any feelings for the woman, only his "plan of action" in his physical lovemaking.

As the sessions progressed, Darren began to realize he was only physically performing when he "made love." As an "assignment," I asked him to find a woman that he wanted to date (he was not dating at that time). Once he found the woman, he could start dating her, but he must agree to avoid any "physical" expressions of love for two months, minimum. He agreed to do so. He was to call me when he started dating again.

Three months later, Darren returned to therapy to tell me he had started dating a young woman, and they had been out on three dates already. He told me that she had started to sexually make moves on him during their first date, and he told her he wanted to get to know her as a person before he became physically involved. She broke out in tears, he related to me, as every man she had ever dated had wanted sex with her on the first date. She was so in agreement with Darren to wait for sex until they had gotten to know each other first and appreciate each other as people of worth and value, and not just for sexual responses. The young woman had also said that she had never dated or been with a young man long enough to appreciate him as a person of value and to emotionally be able to connect with him.

An interesting note about these two young adults is that they both enjoyed the process of getting to know each other on a deeper emotional level. Their level of understanding and trust for each other grew, as did their desire to be physically intimate. Darren came back to see me a year later to update me on his progress. He reported that eventually he and his girlfriend were physically and emotionally intimate with great success. Darren no longer focused on his physical plans for sex, but focused instead on his feelings for her and her feelings of closeness for him. They completely enjoyed each other. Darren had also learned to believe in himself. He feels he has a great future ahead.

Darren's story depicts what can happen to a couple when they learn to emotionally connect. Both Darren and his girlfriend became other-focused, set boundaries, were flexible with each other, had shared personal values, were vulnerable, and trusted each other. Neither wanted a long-term commitment at this time, but they were growing into the realization that this was also an important aspect of a relationship. They also realized that they had a lot to learn about themselves and what they truly wanted in life.

The nine dynamics explored here are nine important ways that a couple can use to grow their emotional feelings for each other.

These dynamics are works in progress and vary in intensity and effectiveness, depending on each person's ability and willingness to incorporate them into his or her ways of interacting with the one he or she loves. Couples must first be aware that these dynamics exist in themselves to a varying degree and are important aspects of one's ability to emotionally love one's partner. Then, the person must be willing to understand the role these dynamics play in one's relationship and be willing to make improvement where needed. Both partners need this willingness.

These dynamics, when properly used and lived, create an emotional feeling of love that naturally draws us to our partner, who also is properly using and living these dynamics. The synergy between the two of you will be rewarding in many ways.

I am realistic enough to know that living these dynamics is not always easy, but keeping them in focus at all times makes this rewarding task easier. Aside from making you emotionally happier with each other, there is an added benefit to being emotionally close—the physical and sexual draw it produces in couples.

I facilitate a lot of marriage therapy where couples have lost their way. They have become emotionally distant and, when this happens, there is usually a drop in sexual activity—sometimes to the point that sexual intimacy stops altogether. They may even be sleeping in separate bedrooms by the time they come to see me.

For each couple, there is a different story; there is a different history. Here are just a few of the reasons couples state as causes for their emotional and physical distance (remembering that there are usually several of these issues going on at the same time):

- One partner feels there is a lack of attention given to him/her. One feels ignored by their spouse at home and out in public.

- One partner feels that he/she is there only to be a sexual outlet for the other partner.

- One partner controls the actions and thoughts of the other partner; his/her way of doing things is the only way.

- Both partners claim that they cannot find a common enjoyable activity to do together.

- Both partners cannot come to an agreement on how to discipline the children.

- One or both partners do not trust that the other partner will not have an affair, that one or both lack the commitment to be monogamous.

- Maybe one of the partners spends too much money that the couple doesn't have, or gambles away their money.

- A partner refuses to work on an addiction.

- One or both partners feel they cannot communicate with the other, even on simple things.

- The partner's family of origin does not accept his/her partner.

- There is a major difference in spiritual values and spiritual practice, which affects the children.

- There are past, unresolved traumas in one or both of the partners that prevent emotional and/or physical intimacy.

- One or both feel they were too young when they married and/or feel they married for the wrong reason.

- One of the partners is in the marriage only for what he/she can get from the other. The partner is never a priority over his/her personal wants and needs.

- There is no feeling of equality.

All of the above issues in marriage do share possible good outcomes if both are willing to make personal changes. By using the nine dynamics and finding new solutions to the unique problems in their relationships, the outcomes take on new levels of intimacy.

The first step in any troubled relationship is to find the true sources of the discord between the two partners. Communication and trust are important here, as well as a commitment to try and work it out.

Once you have discovered the problems, it is now important to find new ways that seem worth a try...these new ways need to be agreeable to both partners, keeping in mind you may need to remind each other of the dynamics of flexibility, other-centeredness, trust, and forgiveness when necessary. Get new input from books, respected people in your lives, professionals in the helping field, your spiritual advisors, and/or any other trusted source. New input is often needed, as we tend to try the same solutions over and over again.

Determine the new, agreed-upon solutions that will be tried. Start the changes. Evaluate their success, and try again if not successful. Some changes are more difficult than others.

All of the marital issues mentioned in this chapter will negatively affect the emotional intimacy levels of the couple, which in turn will affect their physical intimacy levels.

Bridgett and Ted had been married eighteen years. Eighteen years ago when they said, "Yes, I do and forever," they truly did not understand their vow to each other. It probably could have been rewritten to say, "I do...until I can no longer do it, and forever until it is too difficult for one or both of us to continue loving one another." So Ted and Bridgett came to me for marriage therapy, stating that they were finding it difficult to stay committed. They were not real certain if they had the energy to try to make the changes that would help the marriage grow. After all, the passion was gone; their two children—ages twelve and fourteen—were driving them crazy; money was tight; and they couldn't agree upon anything, but they wanted to get help from a professional to help them see if their thinking and feelings about the marriage warranted them going their separate ways.

Therapy began with both of them willing to be flexible and honest in their commitment to try new approaches to their marital issues. As in many marriages, there were issues from each of their histories that often got in the way of their relating. Bridgett's mom had told her to never trust a man; after all, they only wanted you for sex. Ted hated his mom, who always put him down, saying that he would never amount to anything in life. Ted's dad left Ted's mom, as his dad could not tolerate being put down daily by Ted's mom. Bridgett's dad was never home to relate to his children, but Bridgett did love him. Bridgett had been sexually abused by a fourteen-year-old neighborhood boy when she was twelve. Ted had never been sexually intimate nor emotionally close to any woman before he met and married

Bridgett. There were other issues as well in their individual historic that warranted attention.

Both Ted and Bridgett wanted to deal with these issues once they were implicated as having an effect on their marriage. Both were willing to work on themselves as individuals to make each of them a potentially better partner. *Their willingness to individually look at their own issues for the purpose of making a difference in their marriage showed their flexibility, other-centeredness, trust, vulnerability, and commitment to move forward.* They, while in marital therapy, realized that there were strong feelings and good reasons they had been attracted to each other on an emotional level as well as a physical level eighteen years ago. The "glue" to carry on was there. It had been lost, but it was there to retrieve.

Why do the sexual issues seem to get more attention as a reason to seek marital therapy or cause problems in a relationship? One reason may be that sexual issues are generally a composite of other relationship issues, but they are more noticeable and possibly placed on a higher priority list by one or both partners.

The couple, Ted and Bridgett, had not been intimate for the past three years. The sexual issue—the lack of sex—was the compelling force that caused them to seek therapy. They were aware that other issues were at play and felt the need to include them in their therapy goals.

During the course of their therapy, trust, vulnerability, communication, and flexibility became target issues. By working through their willingness to trust in each other and trust that they would work out their differences and be open in communicating their feelings and flexible in resolving their differences, their efforts made them closer than they had ever been with each other. By working on the dynamics in their relationship, they became emotionally and physically more intimate. Their mutual choice to be committed and work it out paid off for them.

To have that physical attraction and intimacy last through the years, the relationship needs the emotional intimacy piece present. The feeling of being wanted, being appreciated as a person of worth and value, and being accepted even though you are not perfect draws you to emotionally want your partner physically. This is true for both men and women.

Men also want to be accepted as persons of worth and value. They want their partners to show them emotional closeness as well as know that their partners want to be with them physically. Often men are accused of not expressing their emotions to the one they love—that physical draw seems to be their only interest. I am sure this can be true in some cases, for both men and women. But, in general, unless blocked by strong past negative events in their lives, men do want to show emotions and be shown emotions in their relationships, some more easily than others. A person's family of origin influences a person's natural ability to express emotions to the one they love. But even taking this history into account, men can and do learn the importance of expressing emotional feelings to their significant others.

Blocks to emotional expressions of feelings can happen to both men and women. When this happens, it definitely can take its toll on the relationship. When there are blocks, using the qualities expressed in the nine dynamics can help the person get to a better emotional way of relating to the one they love.

There are many ways a committed relationship can still fail, but there are many ways to keep a relationship alive and healthy. Use the nine dynamics to help both of you grow in your relationship and to help both of you deepen your emotional and physical levels of love for each other.

Loving more completely and more intimately leads to a better self, to a better relationship, to better family, and to a better world to live in.

QUESTIONS

Physical Intimacy

Are you capable of
being physically inti-
mate with the person
you love?

ALWAYS | | | | | **NEVER**

Is the person you love
capable of being physi-
cally intimate with
you?

ALWAYS | | | | | **NEVER**

Do you both agree
upon the level of
importance of being
physically intimate in
a committed relation-
ship?

ALWAYS | | | | | **NEVER**

Do you both agree
upon the level of
importance in being
emotionally intimate
as well as being physi-
cally intimate?

ALWAYS | | | | | **NEVER**

Can you both openly
discuss your thoughts
and feelings about
being physically inti-
mate?

ALWAYS | | | | | **NEVER**

Do you both agree that
there are no past events
or influences that block
either of you from
being physically inti-
mate?

ALWAYS | | | | | **NEVER**

References

Allen, D. *Contemplation: Intimacy in a Distant World*. McLean, VA: Curtain Call Productions, 2004.

Carlson, J., and L. Sperry. *The Intimate Couple* (1st ed.) New York, NY: Routledge, 1998.

Cloud, H., and J. Townsend. *Boundaries Participant's Guide—Revised: When to Say Yes, How to Say No to Take Control of Your Life*. Grand Rapids, MI: Zondervan, 2007.

Cordova, J. V. *The Marriage Checkup: A Scientific Program for Sustaining and Strengthening Marital Health*. New York, NY: Jason Aronson, 2009.

Corey, G. *Theory and Practice of Group Counseling* (8th ed.) Belmont, CA: Thomson Brooks/Cole, 2011.

Covey, Stephen M. R., with Rebecca R. Merrill. *The Speed of Trust*. New York, NY: Free Press, 2006.

Dowrick, S. *Intimacy and Solitude: Balance, Closeness and Independence*. New York, NY: W.W. Norton, 1996

Fincham, F. D., and S. H. Beach. "Forgiveness and Quality: Precursor or Consequence in Well-Established Relationships?" *Journal of Positive Psychology* 2 (2007): 260–268.

Gerson, M. "The Justice of Intimacy: Beyond the Golden Rule." *Contemporary Psychoanalysis* 43 (2007): 247–260.

Gurtman, M. B. "Trust, Distrust, and Interpersonal Problems: A Circumplex Analysis." *Journal of Personality and Social Psychology* 62 (1992): 989–1002.

Hales, D. *An Invitation to Health: Choosing to Change* (14th ed.) Belmont, CA: Thomson Brooks/Cole, 2008.

Linder, D. *Relational Recovery: Empowering the Transformation of Relationships*. San Francisco, CA: Relationship Vision, 2006.

L'Abate, L. *Personality in Intimate Relationships: Socialization and Psychopathology*. New York, NY: Springer, 2005.

Mellody, P., and L. S. Freundlich. *The Intimacy Factor: The Ground Rules for Overcoming the Obstacles to Truth, Respect, and Lasting Love*. San Francisco, CA: HarperOne, 2004.

Prager, K. J. *The Psychology of Intimacy*. New York, NY: Guilford Press, 1998.

Prilleltensky, I., and O. Prilleltensky. *Promoting Well-Being: Linking Personal, Organizational and Community Change*. New York, NY: Wiley, 2006.

Reevy, G., Y. M. Ozer, and Y. Ito. *Encyclopedia of Emotion, Volume 1*. Westport, CT: Greenwood Press, 2010.

Stuart, R. B. *Helping Couples Change: A Social Learning Approach to Marital Therapy*. New York, NY: Guilford Press, 1981.

Wiley, A. R. "Connecting as a Couple: Communication Skills for Healthy Relationships " *The Forum for Family and Consumer Issues* 12 (2007).

16175796R00073

Made in the USA
Charleston, SC
08 December 2012